J Bio
Fra   Gosda, Randy T.
WITHDRAWN Benjamin
        Franklin

DATE DUE

Benjamin Franklin

A Buddy Book
by
Randy T. Gosda

ABDO
Publishing Company

VISIT US AT
www.abdopub.com

Published by Buddy Books, an imprint of ABDO Publishing Company, 4940 Viking Drive, Suite 622, Edina, Minnesota 55435. Copyright © 2002 by Abdo Consulting Group, Inc. International copyrights reserved in all countries. No part of this book may be reproduced in any form without written permission from the publisher.

Printed in the United States.

Edited by: Christy DeVillier
Contributing Editors: Matt Ray, Michael P. Goecke
Image Research: Deborah Coldiron, Susan Will
Graphic Design: Jane Halbert
Cover Photograph: North Wind Picture Archives
Interior Photographs/Illustrations: North Wind Picture Archives, Library of Congress; Corbis, Deborah Coldiron

Library of Congress Cataloging-in-Publication Data

Gosda, Randy T., 1959-
    Benjamin Franklin / Randy T. Gosda.
        p. cm. — (First biographies. Set II)
    Includes index.
    Summary: Describes the life and notable accomplishments of the eighteenth-century American printer, statesman, writer, and inventor.
    ISBN 1-57765-733-0
    1. Franklin, Benjamin, 1706-1790—Juvenile literature. 2. Statesman—United States—Biography—Juvenile literature. 3. Inventors—United States—Biography—Juvenile literature. 4. Scientists—United States—Biography—Juvenile literature. 5. Printers—United States—Biography—Juvenile literature. [1. Franklin, Benjamin, 1706-1790. 2. Statesmen. 3. Scientists. 4. Printers.] I. Title.

E302.6.F8 G67 2002
973.3'092—dc21
[B]
                                                                    2001034934

Table Of Contents

Who Is Benjamin Franklin?

Many people call Benjamin Franklin the wisest American. This wise American loved his country. Benjamin did a lot to make America a great place to live.

Benjamin Franklin

Growing Up

Benjamin Franklin was born on January 17, 1706, in Boston, Massachusetts. People called him Ben. Ben had 16 brothers and sisters.

At age 10, Ben worked for his father, Josiah. Josiah Franklin was a soap and candle maker. Young Ben did not like making soap and candles. So, he started working for his brother, James.

James was a printer. A printer puts words on paper. James printed his own newspaper. This newspaper was the *New England Courant*.

Benjamin liked printing.

Printing And Writing

When Ben Franklin was 17 years old, he left Boston. By December 1728, he had his own print shop in Philadelphia. He printed his own newspaper, *The Pennsylvania Gazette*. Two years later, Ben married Deborah Read Rogers.

Ben's newspaper was a success. So, he started *Poor Richard's Almanack*. An almanac is a special book with a calendar inside. Ben's almanac was full of jokes, poems, and sayings. Benjamin Franklin is famous for his sayings.

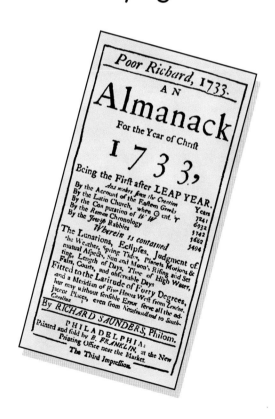

Ben's Philadelphia

Benjamin Franklin helped Philadelphia become a better city. He helped Philadelphia's muddy streets become paved roads. Pavement is the hard covering on a road. Thanks to Ben, Philadelphia's roads had street lights, too.

Ben made Philadelphia a nice place to live.

America's first public library and fire station opened in Philadelphia. This city built a public school and a hospital, too. These things happened because of Benjamin Franklin.

This was Philadelphia's first library.

The Kite Experiment

At age 42, Benjamin Franklin took a break from printing. He began studying new things like electricity. Back then, nobody knew much about electricity. Nobody had electric lights.

Benjamin thought electricity was like lightning. So, he tried an experiment. In 1752, Benjamin Franklin flew a kite during a thunderstorm. He tied a key to the kite string. Lightning struck the kite. Benjamin felt a shock when he touched the key. That was electricity!

Ben's Inventions

Benjamin Franklin's kite experiment helped him build the first lightning rod. A lightning rod keeps buildings safe from lightning. People use lightning rods today.

Lightning rods are on many of today's buildings.

Benjamin Franklin also invented the Franklin stove. This stove was much better than a wood fire. Benjamin's stove used less wood. Yet, it warmed a house well.

Franklin stove

Benjamin needed glasses to see things close up and far away. But he got tired of using two sets of glasses. So, he invented bifocals.

Bifocal glasses are made of two kinds of glass. One kind lets you see things close up. The other kind lets you see things far away.

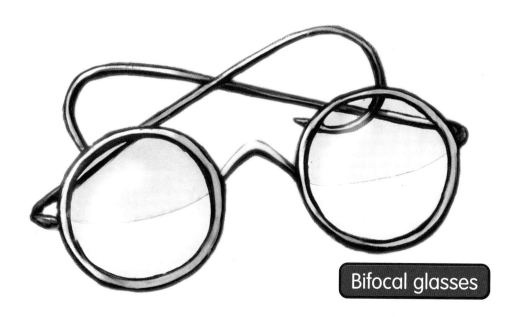

Bifocal glasses

Benjamin was not greedy. He did not want to sell his inventions. Instead, he showed everyone how to build them. Benjamin Franklin's inventions helped many people.

Benjamin shared what he knew about electricity.

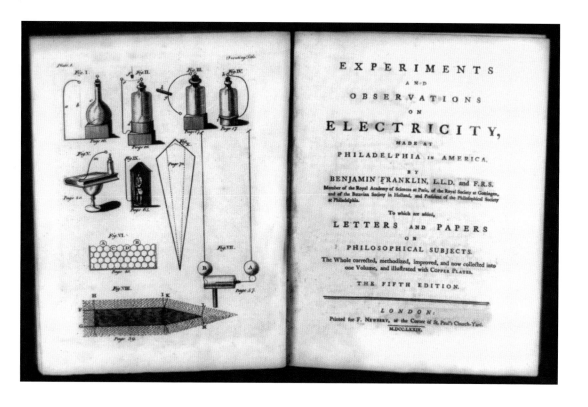

Founding Father

By 1776, America decided to break away from Britain. Benjamin Franklin helped Thomas Jefferson write the Declaration of Independence.

America and Britain went to war. This is what we call the American Revolutionary War.

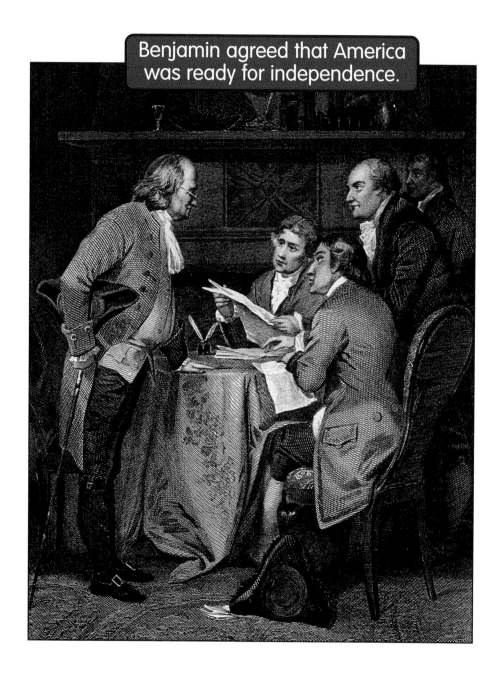

Benjamin agreed that America was ready for independence.

America needed help to win the Revolutionary War. Benjamin Franklin asked France for help. Thanks to Benjamin, France helped America battle the British.

In 1781, America won the Revolutionary War. America became a free country!

Benjamin Franklin won help from France.

In 1787, Benjamin Franklin helped write the United States Constitution. All United States laws are based on the Constitution.

The Wisest American

Benjamin Franklin died on April 17, 1790. He was 84 years old. Thousands of people went to Benjamin's funeral in Philadelphia.

Americans built their country on many of Benjamin Franklin's ideas.

Benjamin Franklin

Benjamin's

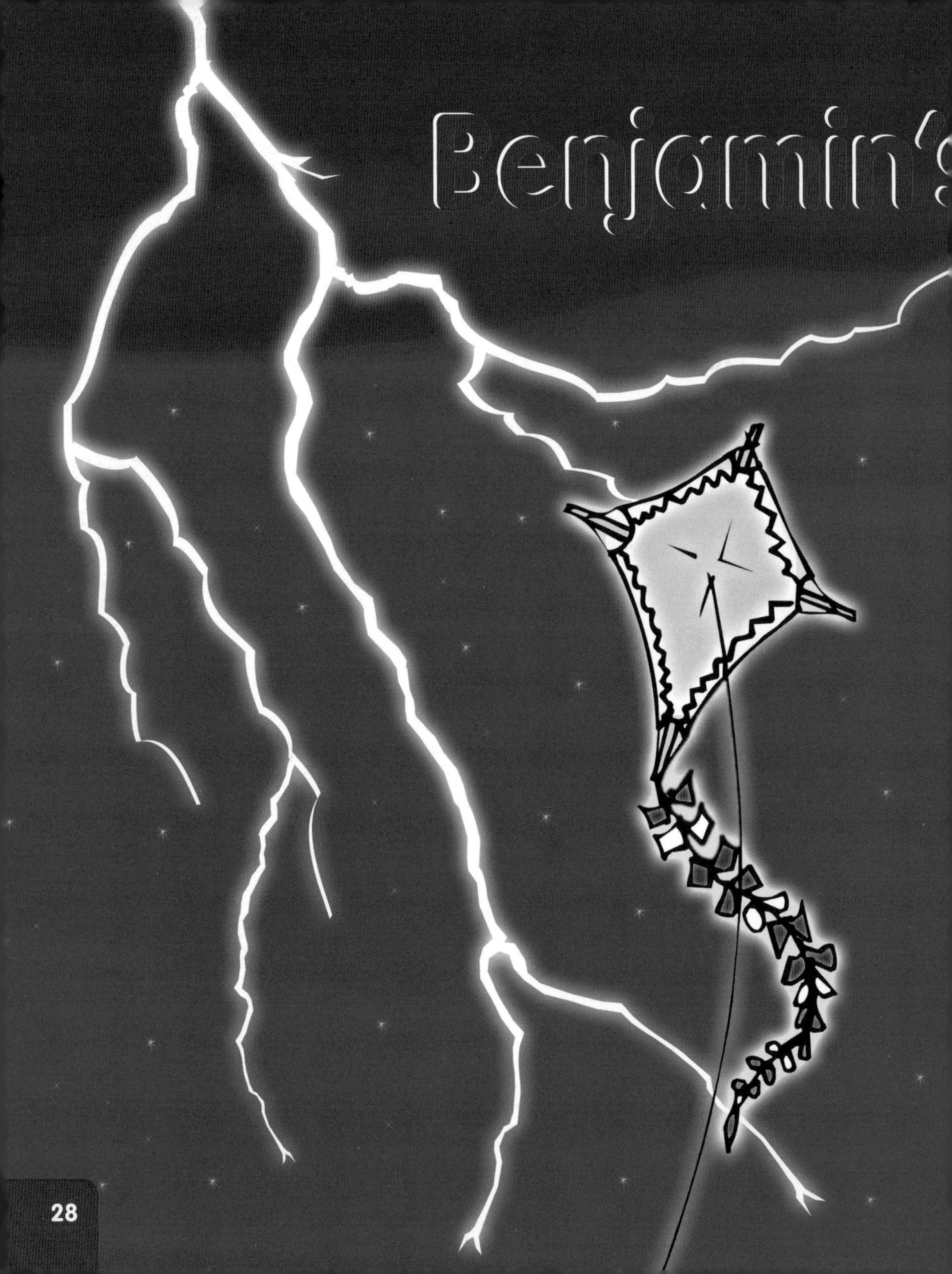

America

Benjamin Franklin did a lot to shape America. Much of what Americans use today comes from Benjamin Franklin.

✓ Sayings like "An apple a day keeps the doctor away."

✓ Inventions like the lightning rod and bifocal glasses.

✓ America's postal (mail) service.

✓ America's basic laws from the U.S. Constitution.

Important Dates

January 17, 1706 Benjamin Franklin is born in Boston, Massachusettes.

1728 Benjamin opens a print shop in Philadelphia.

1731 Benjamin opens America's first public library.

1732 Benjamin begins writing *Poor Richard's Almanack.*

1752 Benjamin discovers electricity in lightning.

1776 Benjamin signs the Declaration of Independence.

1781 America wins the Revolutionary War. A new country is born.

April 17, 1790 Benjamin Franklin dies at the age of 84.

Important Words

almanac a book that gives weather information for each year.

Declaration of Independence an important paper in American history. Americans say they are ready to break away from Britain and rule themselves as a free, or independent, country.

electricity what powers electric things like lights and television.

experiment a kind of test to discover something new.

invent to make something new. People call this new thing an invention.

Web Sites

The World of Benjamin Franklin
http://sln.fi.edu/franklin/
This site describes Franklin's productive life and offers special activities for children.

Ben's Guide to U.S. Government
http://bensguide.gpo.gov/benfranklin/index.html
Learn more about Benjamin Franklin and the U.S. government at this activity-filled site created for kids.

Index